Mange Treatment

and

Emergency Care for

Cats and Dogs

Published to Help Abandoned and Homeless Animals,

Not for Profit

Table of Contents

Introduction

Preparing for a medical emergency involving your pet is always best accomplished before the event takes place. This book is designed to help guide you through the important decisions about first aid, as well as how and when to transport your pet quickly and safely to a veterinary hospital or emergency facility.

Keep this book in your home or car as a quick reference during an emergency.

This book is an emergency preparedness ready-reference for dogs and cats. Wise preventive measures, intelligent use of first aid principles, coupled with recognition of abnormal symptoms and treatment of disorders, diseases, and problems, lead to effective health care. A working knowledge of this information will help you eliminate some potentially dangerous circumstances and help you prepare for emergency situations.

It includes information on what to do and what not to do in specific emergency situations. The authors encourage careful reading and occasional rereading. We have tried to make this book easy to understand, avoiding technical terms as often as possible, but defining them in context when they are necessary.

Boosting the Immune System

Dogs and Cats love getting dirty. They are drawn to dirt and mud like magnets, with no regard for anything. But getting mucky could have a powerful effect on their wellbeing, too. Whether they are chasing a squirrel through a neighbor's yard or climbing a tree, it is always inevitable that their paws become muddy and dirty before the day is over.

Why Do Elephants Take A Mud Bath?

Elephants may look like they are having a lot of fun rolling around in the mud, they probably are, but it serves a critical purpose for them.

As they have minimal hair and sweat glands, they find it difficult to cool off under the harsh African sun. The mud not only cools them down and provides a protective layer on their body to shield them from serious illnesses such as mange and scabies, it also protects them from insect bites and the sun. Their skin looks very tough, but it is very sensitive, and can get sunburnt!

Elephants prepare the mud for their baths in two ways. One is to kick their foot in the water to stir up the mud and mix it with the water; the other is to churn the mud with their tusks or trunk up from the bottom when bathing elephants will either roll around in the mud or spray themselves with it using their trunk.

So the act of bathing and mudding is a natural behavior that elephants use to cool off and protect themselves from the sun. Mudding is not only beneficial because of the chance to cool off – but that certain natural materials, contain surprisingly powerful microorganisms whose positive impact on health we are only beginning to fully understand.

Mental restoration

Many of the psychological benefits of outdoor play are already well established. Our brains evolved in natural landscapes, and our perceptual systems are particularly well suited to wild outdoor spaces. The outdoors not only beneficial for your pet, but also for your children. Outdoor play can offer valuable learning experiences. For example, the act of molding and kneading materials like mud or sand can help children develop the way their senses and movement interact, known as sensorimotor development. This allows the child to gradually understand his or her bodily signals.

Such activities – away from the house or – may also help your pet or child find ways to cope with an illness or emotions. So-called "sand tray therapy", which involves using sand and miniature figurines to express one's thoughts and feelings, is an accepted form of counselling for children who are struggling to verbalize their emotional state.

When it comes to the physical health, the most obvious advantage of outdoor play may be the exercise. Any creature may find it easier to build up strength and stamina in a large open space resulting in reduced risk of heart disease and obesity.

Often it is non-infectious organisms that make you sick. These "old friends" have been around for much of our evolutionary history. They are mostly harmless, and train the immune system to moderate its activity, rather than over-reacting to any potential invader.

Importantly, we often meet these old friends whenever we spend time in nature. With increased urbanization, and reduced outdoor play, many pets and children now lack that exposure – meaning that their immune systems are more sensitive to any threat, and more likely to go into overdrive.

Friendly microbes in the gut can improve the health, and they may also act through the skin. People and pets that grow up on farms are less likely to develop asthma, allergies, or auto-immune disorders because of the exposure to a more diverse range of organisms in the rural environment that had encouraged more effective regulation of the immune system. Much of the healthy stimulation, afforded by these bugs, is thought to come through the digestive system – it is now well known that friendly microbes in the gut can improve the health in multiple ways. But they may also act on and through the skin. The outer layer of the body hosts many species of microbes.

Most surprisingly, friendly bugs from nature can even moderate the body's response to stress. When a person or a pet feels vulnerable and threatened, the immune system starts raising bodily temperature. Such inflammation is one of the first defenses against infection, this response evolved as a way of preparing the body for a potential physical injury from the threat we were facing. Remarkably, children and pets that spend the majority of their childhoods in a rural setting tend to show a more muted response to stressful events, with the reduced expression of inflammatory molecules compared with those who had grown up in cities. Chronic bodily inflammation can contribute to a range of conditions. It appears to increase the risk of depression, for example. Most creatures that grow up in cities are kind of 'walking time bombs', in terms of their inflammation. Some scientists have also expressed considerable excitement about the role of "helminthes" – soil-dwelling parasites such as roundworm – largely due to the moderated immune response they trigger in their hosts.

People and pets that are infected with helminthes seem to have a lower risk of inflammatory bowel diseases. Thus mud baths and thermal mineral water baths – may improve the health by introducing beneficial organisms to the skin's microbial communities. Many species are responsible for the benefits, including Staphylococcus epidermidis, which has been shown to have anti-inflammatory effects.

Given the importance of early exposure to friendly bacteria, many scientists are investigating the benefits of interventions that encourage greater contact with nature in childhood. The act of "forest bathing" – gentle meditative walks through the woods – has been shown to improve the overall health. By touching the trees, the leaves and the soil, friendly organisms are picked up that enrich the skin and the body.

What is First Aid?

First aid is the immediate care given to a pet who has been injured or is suddenly taken ill. The immediate care includes:

Primary Survey and Resuscitation

The primary survey is the first impression the first aid provider has of the situation, and the immediate action that is taken. A well-informed owner will be able to make a quick assessment of the scene and a quick examination of the victim. Immediate attention is given to the animal's level of consciousness, airway patency, breathing, and circulatory functions (including pulse). Resuscitation is the prompt treatment of life-threatening problems.

Secondary Survey and Definitive First Aid

The secondary survey consists of an examination and assessment of the animal's eyes, ears, nose, neck, chest, abdomen, back, extremities, and rectal temperature and the procedures to stabilize and protect the animal from further harm.

Transport

Many emergencies will require professional help. Knowledge of the proper way to transport the pet to a veterinary medical facility for professional care can prevent further injury, protect the owner from dangerous situations, and allow for timely care.

First Aid Kit

Emergency supplies are a necessity. The following list will help you assemble the resources you need.

- 1" and 2" adhesive tape

- 2" roll gauze (for muzzle)

- Newspaper

- Rectal thermometer

- Chlorhexidine or povidone iodine (antiseptic)

- Elizabethan collar

- Eye wash (saline in a squirt bottle)

- Isopropyl alcohol 3% hydrogen peroxide (or syrup of ipecac)

- 2" and 4" gauze

- 3" x 3" or 4" x 4" gauze pads

- Scissors - cotton balls and pledgets

- Blanket with heat pack

- Flat transport surface

- Plastic food wrap (e.g., Saran- Wrap)

- Petroleum or K-Y jelly

- Ice pack

- Activated charcoal

- Tweezers

- Bulb syringe

A complete first aid kit for your pet is a must.

Preparedness Phone Numbers

In a convenient location, make a list of important phone numbers that includes the phone numbers of the following:

- Your veterinarian

- Your veterinarian's emergency (after-hours) number

- Your nearest 24-hour veterinary emergency facility

- Your local poison control center

- National poison control centers

Emergency numbers should be kept near your phone for easy access. Update numbers as necessary.

General Directions for First Aid

A wide variety of problems arise that require first aid skills. Decisions and actions vary according to the circumstances, including:

• Scene of the accident

• Emergency equipment available

• Species, size, age, temperament, and condition of the animal requiring first aid

• Your emotional condition

• Other emotionally stable people available to help you.

First aid begins with a quick but careful survey of the scene. Then quick decisions need to be made, depending on the circumstances.

• Make sure the accident scene is safe before proceeding. Take steps to prevent further injury to you or your pet.

• Enlist the help of others.

• Call, or have someone call, your veterinarian or the emergency veterinary center. (Keep those phone numbers handy at all times!) Describe the animal, give a short description of what happened and what has been done. Give your name and telephone number. Don't hang up until the professionals have told you what to do.

• Administer essential first aid. Carefully transport the animal to the veterinary facility for examination if there is any question as to the seriousness of the injury or sudden illness. It is highly recommended to telephone first in all but the most life- threatening situations.

Muzzling

When attending a dog that has been injured, it is important that the first aid provider takes steps to prevent bite wounds inflicted by the animal being treated. Many dogs, even the family pet, may bite when hurt or frightened. A muzzle is an excellent way to prevent being bitten while rendering first aid. Commercial muzzles are best, as many of them can be used without interfering with breathing; the problem is they are not always available during a crisis.

If a muzzle is not available, the first aid provider must improvise. To make a muzzle, get a rope, cord or other similar strong material (such as a necktie or a belt). Wrap the cord or rope two or three times around the muzzle, being careful not to wrap the material too close to the soft, fleshy part of the nose. The muzzle must be applied to the bony part of the nose to avoid interfering with breathing. Bring the ends up past the ears and tie the securely behind the head.

These muzzles cannot be used on dogs who are having difficulty breathing, are unconscious, or have an injury to the mouth. They're also not indicated for short nose breeds (e.g., Chinese Pug, Pekingese, Bulldog).

Some injured dogs may vomit. If the dog appears to become nauseated or begins to retch, the muzzle should be removed at once.

Primary Survey and Resuscitation

The primary survey is often referred to as the ABC's of first aid, indicating the following areas of emphasis:

- "A"irway

- "B"reathing & "B"leeding

- "C"ardiovascular (which includes heart function, pulse, and capillary refill time)

In most cases, the pet owner will administer a minimal amount of first aid and then transport the animal to a veterinary facility. Occasionally it is necessary to continue the care with some additional procedures, particularly if veterinary help will not be available for some period of time. Please read the following sections carefully. "A"irway, "B"reathing, and "C"ardiovascular are covered in the sections on CPR and Shock. The sections on bleeding and bandaging will cover information on controlling bleeding. First aid for fractures is covered in the section on splints. First aid treatment for poisoning and choking cases is described in poisoning and choking.

Safe Rescue

In order to administer first aid to an animal, it may be necessary to remove him (and yourself) from a road or a highway. Remove your pet from the highway only after making sure it is safe to retrieve him. Direct traffic if necessary. If the pet appears likely to bite because of pain or excitement, cover the pet (including the head) with a blanket and/or muzzle the pet before handling. If there is any evidence of head, neck, or spinal injury (such as inability to move the rear legs), you should move the animal onto a flat surface for transport rather than picking him up. Make sure to secure an accident scene before attempting a rescue.

Mange Treatment

Mange is a skin disease that affects mammals caused by microscopic mites that burrow into skin. Mange will make an animal suffer then it will kill them. It can only be treated by medication. The best treatment and medication was developed by Noaha, An Animal Rescue Shelter. You can buy the medication from them. Do not overdose or underdose. Tell them if it is for a cat, dog, cow, or a horse. Send $39.95 check to: Noaha, Box 55573, Houston, Texas 77255

Administer (inject) into back thigh leg using the syringe sent to you. If you catch the illness early and get your pet treated right away, there is a good chance of recovery. Give pet plenty of water and food and gently clean fur and skin with a clean warm cloth each day.

Abscess

A localized accumulation of pus, usually caused by an infection introduced from an animal bite or other penetrating wound. It may appear as a painful swelling or, if it has ruptured, as a draining wound.

What to Do

• If it has ruptured, clean the wound with soap (not detergent) and water. Rinse well and pat dry. Repeat several times a day.

• If there is swelling, apply warm, moist compresses for 10 to 15 minutes. Repeat 3 or 4 times daily.

• Abscesses should be examined by a veterinarian within 24 hours.

What NOT to Do

• Do not attempt to open the abscess yourself.

• Do not apply medicines, potions, or home remedies unless directed to by a veterinarian.

Abscesses are a frequent problem in cats, especially unneutered males who get into territorial or breeding disputes.

During these disputes, the pet may receive a bite or a scratch. If the wound becomes infected, an abscess may form within a day or two. Neutering your male cat will reduce his "need" to fight. Without the influence of male hormones he will mark out a much smaller territory and will be less likely to engage in fights over a female.

Bandaging

We use bandages for several reasons: to protect wounds from the environment, protect the environment from wounds, and to discourage the pet from licking or irritating a wound. They may be applied as support for strains or sprains and to prevent motion. Proper application is important.

Cleaning the Wound

The process of bandaging begins with careful cleaning of the wound. All dried blood, dirt, and debris should be washed away using mild soap and copious amounts of water. Hair should be clipped away so that it cannot lie in the wound, and, if possible, the area should be patted dry.

The first step in proper bandaging is making sure the wound is clean.

The Contact Layer

After cleaning the wound, the contact layer is the first layer applied. Ideally, this layer should:

- Be sterile and inert.

- Stay in close contact with, but not stick to, the wound.

- Be very absorbent.

- Be free of particles or fibers that might shed into the wound.

- Conform to all shapes. Allow drainage to pass to the next layer without becoming wet.

- Minimize pain.

A Telfa-Pad, available at most pharmacies, comes closest to meeting these requirements. After cleaning the wound, place the contact layer over the wound. It is desirable to apply an antibiotic ointment (such as Neosporin) to the pad, but this is not absolutely necessary. Frequent bandage changes are more important. After cleaning the wound, a clean Telfa-Pad should be applied over the area.

The Absorbent Layer

After the contact layer is in place, apply the second (absorbent) layer to hold the contact layer snugly, but not tightly, over the wound. This layer is usually a cotton or dacron material which comes in various widths.

Generally, 1-inch rolls are used for small limbs and the tail, 2-inch rolls are for medium-sized legs, and the 3- and 4-inch rolls are for large legs and the body. It is important to use the proper size. Materials that are too narrow often cause a tourniquet effect, especially if the wound causes swelling.

If materials are too wide, they are difficult to apply smoothly. Any wrinkles or ridges may cause the bandage to become uncomfortable for your pet. Uneven pressure may cause necrosis (tissue death) of the underlying tissues. Begin with just enough absorbent layer to hold the contact layer in place. If the wound is on a leg or the tail, proceed by wrapping from the toes or the tip of the tail towards the body. If you begin at the top of the leg or the tail, the bandage is more likely to restrict blood flow and cause swelling, which may cause tissue damage. Apply several layers of absorbent material, which will soak up the fluid from the wound and increase the patient's comfort by cushioning the wound.

Make sure the material you use as the absorbent layer is the proper width, and wrap from the toes or tail tip towards the body.

The Outer Layer

Finally, apply the outer (tertiary) layer, usually made up of porous adhesive tape or elastic tape (i.e., Elastikon, Vetrap). Wrapped from the toes towards the body, this layer should also be smooth and snug. Do not pull elastic tapes to their limits, as this will interfere with circulation and result in bandage failure. The tape should be in contact with the skin (hair) at the bandage margins, anchoring the bandage so it will not slip.

The outer layer of a bandage should be applied smoothly and snugly, but not tight enough to cutoff blood circulation.

Bandage Changes

Bandages should be checked frequently for any signs of swelling discoloration or coolness of the skin, odor, or saturation of the bandage material. The bandage should be changed whenever any of the above are noticed or any time it appears to be uncomfortable for the pet. Wounds that are draining heavily may require bandage changes every 1 or 2 hours. Bandages over wounds with little or no drainage should be changed every 24 hours.

Bee Stings / Insect Bites

Any insect or spider can cause problems if they bite or sting your pet. A bite or sting causes swelling, redness, and itching. Certain stings can cause your pet to "faint" (see section on fainting) or cause an alarming swelling in the face.

What to Do:

•   If the stinger can be found, pull it out with tweezers by grasping the stinger itself, located below the venom sac. If the sting just happened, don't put pressure on the venom sac, as that would "inject" more of the venom into the pet.

•   Apply cool compresses to the area.

•   To help neutralize some of the acidic venom, apply a paste mixture of baking soda and water to the sting area.

What NOT to Do:

•   Do not administer any medications without first contacting your veterinarian. Bear in mind the veterinarian will likely need to examine your pet before recommending medications.

Bleeding

Pets often suffer blood loss as a result of trauma. If bleeding is severe or continuous, the animal may lose enough blood to cause shock (loss of as little as 2 teaspoons per pound of body weight may cause shock). Emergencies may arise that require the owner to control the bleeding, even if it is just during transport of the animal to the veterinary facility. Pet owners should know how to stop hemorrhage (bleeding) if their pet is injured.

Techniques to Stop External Bleeding

The following techniques are listed in order of preference.

Direct Pressure

Gently press a compress (a pad of clean cloth or gauze) over the bleeding absorbing the blood and allowing it to clot. Do not disturb blood clots after they have formed.

If blood soaks through, do not remove the pad; simply add additional layers of cloth and continue the direct pressure more evenly. The compress can be bound in place using bandage material which frees the hands of the first provider for other emergency actions. In the absence of a compress, a bare hand or finger can be used.

Direct pressure on a wound is the most preferable way to stop bleeding.

Elevation

If there is a severely bleeding wound on the foot or leg, gently elevate the leg so that the wound is above the level of the heart.

Elevation uses the force of gravity to help reduce blood pressure in the injured area, slowing the bleeding. Elevation is most effective in larger animals with longer limbs where greater distances from wound to heart are possible.

Direct pressure with compresses should also be maintained to maximize the use of elevation.

Elevation of a limb combined with direct pressure is an effective way to stop bleeding.

Pressure on the Supplying Artery

If external bleeding continues following the use of direct pressure and elevation, finger or thumb pressure over the main artery to the wound is needed. Apply pressure to the femoral artery in the groin for severe bleeding of a rear leg; to the brachial artery in the inside part of the upper front leg for bleeding of a front leg; or to the caudal artery at the base of the tail if the wound is on the tail. Continue application of direct pressure. Place Pressure Above and Below the Bleeding Wound. This can also be used in conjunction with direct pressure. Pressure above the wound will help control arterial bleeding. Pressure below the wound will help control bleeding from veins.

Tourniquet

Use of a tourniquet is dangerous and it should be used only for a severe, life-threatening hemorrhage in a limb (leg or tail) not expected to be saved. A wide (2-inch or more) piece of cloth should be used to wrap around the limb twice and tied into a knot. A short stick or similar object is then tied into the knot as well. Twist the stick to tighten the tourniquet until the bleeding stops. Secure the stick in place with another piece of cloth and make a written note of the time it was applied. Loosen the tourniquet for 15 to 20 seconds every 20 minutes. Remember this is dangerous and will likely result in disability or amputation.

Use of a tourniquet should only be employed as a last-resort, life-saving measure!

Internal Bleeding

Internal bleeding is a life-threatening condition, but it is not obvious like external bleeding. Any bleeding which is visible is external.

Internal bleeding occurs inside the body and will not be seen. There are, however, external signs of internal bleeding:

• The pet is pale (check the gums or eyelids).

• The pet is cool on the legs, ears, or tail.

• The pet is extremely excited or unusually subdued.

If any of these signs are evident, the pet should be immediately transported to a veterinary facility for professional help. Remember: internal bleeding is not visible on the outside.

Bloat

A life-threatening condition in which the stomach fills with air (dilatation) and, or twists upon itself (volvulus).

What to Do

• Transport to a veterinary hospital or emergency facility immediately. This condition requires professional assistance in all cases.

What **NOT** to Do

• Do not attempt to relieve the gas from the stomach.

• Do not give anything by mouth.

It is imperative that this condition be recognized early. Your pet may not have a bloated appearance. Signs of bloat include:

• Drooling of saliva

• Frequent retching and attempts to vomit (occasionally victims may be able to regurgitate a pool of foamy saliva)

• Anxiousness, restlessness, and pacing

• Depression and shock

Much has been learned about bloat in the past decade. Only a few years ago, a diagnosis of bloat was almost always a death sentence, as only 25% survived. Today the survival rate is better than 80%. Part of the reason for this is increased owner awareness. The earlier the veterinarian gets started with treatment, the better chance there is for survival.

Extremely aggressive medical and surgical intervention early in the course of the disease has the most dramatic impact on overall treatment success.

Burns

Any injury of tissue caused by heat, flame, chemicals, or electricity.

What to Do

- Extinguish all flames.

- For thermal or electrical burns, immediately apply cold water compresses to the site of the injury, changing them frequently as necessary to keep the site cool and wet. Continue this for at least 30 minutes.

- For chemical burns, see the chemical injuries section.

- Transport your pet to a veterinary facility as soon as possible.

What **NOT** to Do

- Do not apply ointments.

- Do not delay seeking veterinary attention.

- Do not attempt to remove burned hair or skin yourself.

Cardiopulmonary Resuscitation (CPR)

Cardiopulmonary resuscitation (CPR) is the treatment required to save an animal (or human) life when he or she has suffered respiratory and/or cardiac arrest. CPR consists of two parts:

Rescue breathing and chest compressions.

These two techniques combine to keep the lungs supplied with oxygen and keep blood circulating, carrying oxygen to the other parts of the body.

Basic CPR is CPR performed by trained bystanders at the scene of the arrest.

Advanced CPR is CPR performed by trained teams of professionals. Basic CPR is the most important, and will be described in this section.

All tissues require a steady source of oxygen. If the source is interrupted for only a few minutes, irreversible damage may be done. If an arrest occurs, basic CPR must be initiated at the scene.

Basic CPR: Rescue Breathing

Make Certain the Animal is Actually Arrested and Unconscious

Talk to the animal first. Gently touch and attempt to awaken the pet. You could be seriously injured should you attempt to perform CPR on a pet who was only sleeping heavily and was startled awake.

Ensure an Open Airway

Extend the head and neck and pull the tongue forward.

Look in the mouth and remove any saliva or vomitus. If it is too dark to see into the mouth, sweep your finger deep into the mouth and even into the throat to remove any vomitus or foreign body. Be aware of a hard, smooth, bone-like structure deep in the throat. This is likely to be the hyoid apparatus (Adam's apple). Serious injury could result if you pull on the hyoid apparatus.

Observe for Effective Breathing

Sometimes an animal will begin to breathe spontaneously when the head is put in the position discussed above (head and neck extended, tongue pulled forward). Watch for the rise and fall of the chest while listening closely for sounds of breathing. If no breathing is evident in 10 seconds, begin rescue breathing.

Begin Rescue Breathing

Rescue breathing is performed by covering the animal's nose with your mouth and forcefully blowing your breath into his lungs. In cats and small dogs, you must hold the corners of the mouth tightly closed while you force the air in.

In larger dogs, the tongue should be pulled forward and the mouth and lips held shut using both hands cupped around the muzzle. Force the air into the lungs until you see the chest expand. Take your mouth away when the chest has fully expended. The lungs will deflate on their own. Air should be forced into the animal's lungs until you see the chest expand.

Give 3 to 5 Full Breaths

After several breaths are given, stop for a few seconds to recheck for breathing and heart function. If the pet is still not breathing, continue rescue breathing 20-25 times per minute in cats or small dogs, or 12-20 times per minute in medium or large dogs.

Push down on the stomach area every few seconds to help expel the air that may have blown into the stomach. If the stomach is allowed to distend with air, the pressure will make the rescue breathing efforts less effective.

If Breathing is Shallow or Non-existent and the animal is still unconscious, continue rescue breathing 10 to 15 times per minute and transport the animal to the nearest veterinary facility.

Basic CPR: Chest Compressions

After Giving 3 to 5 Breaths, Check for a Pulse. If no pulse is detectable, begin chest compressions.

In Small Dogs or Cats

Squeeze the chest using one or both hands around the chest. Depress the rib cage circumferentially. Do this 100 to 150 times per minute.

In Large Dogs

Compress the chest wall with one or two hands, depending on the size of the dog (and the size of the rescuer). If the dog is on her side, place the hand(s) on the side of the chest wall where it is widest. If the dog is on her back, place the hand(s) on the sternum (breastbone). Depress the rib cage or sternum 1.5 to 4 inches, depending on the dog's size. Do this 80 to 120 times per minute.

Coordinate Rescue Breathing and Chest Compressions

Give breaths during the compressions, if possible. If it is not possible to give breaths during the compressions, give two breaths after every 12 compressions.

When Two or More Rescuers are Working Together

Rescue breathing should be given during every second or third heart compression.

Continue CPR Until

• You become exhausted and can't continue.

• You get the animal transported to a veterinary facility and professionals can take over. The pulse is palpable or heartbeats are felt and they are strong and regular. In the vast majority of cases, artificial ventilations will continue to be required for a period of time, even though heart function has returned. This is due to nervous system depression secondary to the arrest.

All resuscitated animals should be transported to a veterinary facility for further examination and care!

Secondary Survey

The secondary survey is performed once resuscitation measures have been successfully performed or when it is decided that resuscitation measures are not required. In some circumstances (because of ongoing resuscitation), the secondary survey is never completed and the animal is transported directly to the veterinarian or emergency hospital during resuscitation.

A general examination (from the tip of the nose to the end of the tail) should be performed. Determine and record:

- Pulse rate and character

- Respiratory rate and character

- Mucous membrane color

- Capillary refill time

- Rectal temperature.

Examine the eyes, ears, nose, neck, mouth (if possible), chest, abdomen, back, pelvis, legs, and tail.

First aid treatment should be performed as necessary during transport to the veterinarian.

Taking and recording your pet's pulse is an important part of the secondary survey.

Chemical Injuries

Injury to tissue caused by contact with harmful chemicals such as lye, acids, and strong cleaning supplies.

What to Do

• Wash the contaminated area with large volumes of flowing water for at least 15 minutes.

• In the case of dry chemicals, brush them away carefully, taking special care to protect your and your pet's eyes, nose, and mouth.

• If the chemical is in the eye, flush the eye with large volumes of water or saline for 15 minutes. See below for saline recipe)

• Seek veterinary attention as soon as possible.

What **NOT** to Do

• Do not apply "neutralizing agents" to the skin or eyes. They can cause a chemical reaction that produces heat and cause further injury to tissues.

• Do not immerse your pet in "non-flowing" water if a dry chemical has spilled on him. These dry chemicals are usually activated by water. The water must be flowing in order to rinse the chemical away.

Pure water can be quite irritating to the eyes and raw skin. It is much more comfortable for your pet if you use saline: simply dissolve 2 teaspoons of table salt in one quart of water (metric: 9 grams of salt in 1 liter of water).

Dehydration

Excess loss of water from the body or inappropriate intake of water into the body.

What to Do

•   If moderate or severe, seek veterinary attention.

•   If mild, give frequent, small amounts of water by mouth.

•   Move the pet to a cool (not cold) environment to help reduce panting.

What NOT to Do

•   Do not allow the pet to have immediate free access to water or other liquid.

•   Do not feed him any dry food.

Dehydration often accompanies vomiting, diarrhea, hypothermia, fever, no access to water, and other conditions. It can be detected by several tests:

Mouth: Are the tongue and gums moist or dry? If they are dry, the pet may be dehydrated. Is the saliva thick or ropy? Normally, saliva is quite watery and hardly noticeable.

Eyes: Are they normal, or do they sink into the sockets? Sunken or dry eyes may indicate dehydration, and warrant veterinary attention.

Skin: Do the skin turgor test outlined in the Physical Exam Checklist. If the skin is slow to return to position, the animal is at least 5% dehydrated. If the skin does not return fully to its position, the animal is 10% to 12% dehydrated and is likely in critical condition.

Diarrhea and Vomiting

Diarrhea is the frequent evacuation of watery stools. Vomiting is the forceful expulsion of stomach contents through the mouth.

What to Do

- Remove all food and water.

- Check for signs of dehydration.

- If the diarrhea and/or vomiting continues or the pet acts ill, seek veterinary attention. Diarrhea and vomiting can quickly lead to serious fluid loss and electrolyte imbalance, especially in the very young and the very old.

•   If no vomiting occurs for 6 to 8 hours, begin to give small amounts of clear liquids (water, Gatorade, Pedialyte, or other electrolyte solution) frequently. A rule of thumb is to give 1 teaspoon per pound of body weight every 2 or 3 hours throughout the day and night.

•   Isolate the sick pet from other pets.

What **NOT** to Do

•   Do not medicate your pet without talking to your veterinarian.

•   Do not allow the pet to eat or drink anything until there has been no vomiting for 6 to 8 hours.

Vomiting and diarrhea are associated with a host of problems which are referred to collectively as gastroenteritis. Some cases are quite severe (e.g., poisoning), and some are not (e.g., dietary indiscretion). If fever is present, infection may be a cause.

Most infections which cause diarrhea and vomiting are contagious, so it is wise to assume that other pets might be vulnerable if they are exposed. If your pet is not feeling well and has vomiting and/or diarrhea, he should see a veterinarian.

Difficult Birth

At the beginning of labor, the contractions may be infrequent, weak, or incomplete. The female may continue for up to 3 hours before a veterinary examination is necessary. If the contractions are frequent, regular, and strong, and no young is produced in 15 to 30 minutes, the pet should be taken to a veterinarian.

What to Do

•   If a baby is visible in the birth canal and appears stuck, gently grasp the foot or feet. With a steady motion gently pull on the baby only when the female is contracting. If the baby does not come out easily, transport the pet to a veterinarian.

• When the baby is born, it will likely be covered in a membrane. If the mother doesn't remove it, tear this membrane and remove it from the head region of the baby.

• If the mother doesn't remove the umbilical cord (or is being rough with it), tie it with a piece of string one fourth of an inch from the baby's abdomen. Then cut the cord one half of an inch from the abdomen with a sharp scissor. Apply iodine to the stump.

• Keep the babies warm. It is best to leave them with their mother, but sometimes she doesn't stay with them. In this instance, put a milk bottle filled with warm water near the babies. A hot water bottle works, as does a heating pad (set on low only!) Allow room for the babies to move toward or away from the heat source.

What NOT to Do

• Do not put your fingers in the birth canal as you may cause infection.

- Do not forcibly attempt to remove a baby.

- Do not assist delivery by pulling on the head of a baby.

- Do not lift the baby by the umbilical cord.

- Do not use a heating pad on a high or medium setting.

- Most kitten and puppy births go smoothly, with the mother doing all the work. The babies contentedly nurse on the mother soon after birth.

Electrocution

In order to avoid injury to yourself, it is imperative that you do not touch the pet until the electrical source has been turned off or moved.

What to Do

- Unplug the electrical cord or shut off the electricity.

• If this is not possible, use a dry wooden broom or other non-conductive object to move the pet away from the source of the electricity.

• Check for breathing and pulse. Begin CPR if necessary.

• If the pet is breathing, check its mouth for burns. Apply cool compresses to burns.

• Cover the pet with a blanket to prevent heat loss.

• Seek veterinary attention as soon as possible.

What NOT to Do

• Do not fail to get the pet examined even though she seems perfectly normal after being separated from the source of electricity.

• Do not give any medications or liquids unless instructed to by a veterinarian.

Any animal that has suffered electrocution should be taken to a veterinarian, even if there are no apparent complications. Electrocution is a life-threatening emergency.

It may cause abnormal electrical activity of the heart or a build-up of fluid in the lungs which could be fatal hours after the shock.

Eye Injuries

Any condition that causes your pet to squint or protect his eye; any suspected trauma to the eye; any abnormal appearance of the eyeball; any time the eyelid cannot cover the eyeball, these are potential emergencies and veterinary attention should be sought immediately.

What to Do

•   If the eye has been dislocated from the socket (proptosis) or the lids cannot close over the eyeball, keep the eyeball moist with contact lens wetting solution, K-Y jelly, water, or moist compresses. An old home remedy that works is keeping the eye moist with pure honey.

•   If an irritating chemical or other product accidentally gets into the eye, flush it with running water, or water (or saline) squeezed from a sponge for a minimum of 15 minutes.

(Saline: dissolve 2 teaspoons of table salt in I quart of water)

• Always seek veterinary attention immediately. Eyes are quite fragile and just a few minutes could mean the difference between sight and blindness.

What **NOT** to Do

• Do not attempt to treat the eyes, or remove a foreign object, yourself.

• Do not try to push a proptosed eyeball back into the socket. This must be done under anesthesia so as not to cause damage to the eyeball's interior.

Fainting/Dizziness (Syncope)

Fainting is the sudden loss of consciousness or a sudden and marked weakness. It may be associated with anything from low blood sugar to severe heart disease. Bee stings are frequently a cause of syncope.

What to Do

•   Immediately position the pet with the head down and the hind quarters elevated.

•   Cover the pet with a blanket to preserve body heat.

•   If the pet vomits, make sure he does not inhale any of the vomitus into his lungs.

•   Seek veterinary attention.

What NOT to Do

•   Do not administer anything by mouth. It can be aspirated into the lungs and cause serious problems.

•   Do not slap the pet or douse him with cold water trying to shock him into consciousness.

•   Do not fail to seek veterinary attention just because the animal recovered quickly and seems fine now. Several of the conditions that cause syncope are extremely serious.

Fever

Fever is the elevation of body temperature in response to infection or inflammation (Also see hypothermia).

What to Do

•   Take and record the rectal temperature. If it is above 103 degrees, you should call your veterinarian. Temperature elevations above 106 degrees are life threatening and demand immediate attention.

•   If the animal's temperature is over 105 degrees, mix one half water and one half rubbing alcohol. Sponge this on the pet and direct a fan on the moistened area.

•   Apply a cool pack or an alcohol and water compress to the top of the head to help protect the brain.

•   Encourage (but do not force) your pet to drink small, frequent quantities of water.

What NOT to Do

•   Be careful not to over treat! Discontinue cooling once the rectal temperature reaches 103 degrees.

•   Do not give aspirin or other drugs. Many of these drugs are poisonous to pets.

When a pet is lethargic, depressed, shivering a lot, or there is any other reason to suspect that he is not well (not eating, or is vomiting, coughing, has a running nose), you should suspect fever. The only way to confirm this is to take the animal's temperature using a medical thermometer. Detailed information on taking rectal temperature can be found in the temperature section of the Physical Exam Checklist.

First Aid for Choking

Choking is interference with breathing caused by foreign material in, or compression on, the trachea (windpipe).

If the Pet is Unconscious

Perform a Finger Sweep

Open your pet's mouth and perform a finger sweep by placing your finger along the inside of the mouth, sliding it down toward the center of the throat over the base of the tongue and gently "sweeping" toward the center to remove any foreign material. Warning: there is a structure deep in the throat (the Adam's Apple) that feels like a smooth bone. Do not attempt to pull it out!

Begin Rescue Breathing

Rescue breathing is described in the CPR section. If air is not entering the lungs, slap the pet's chest wall firmly or perform the Heimlich maneuver by putting the pet on its back, placing your hands over the abdomen near the bottom of its rib cage, and gently, but firmly thrusting toward the spine. Perform a finger sweep and begin rescue breathing.

Repeat until the foreign body is clear and the lungs can be inflated. Transport to the veterinarian.

If the Pet is Conscious

Stay calm and try to keep the pet calm. If the pet is overheated, wrap him in a wet towel, and transport him to the veterinarian. Perform a finger sweep only if it will not excite the pet.

Frequently, pet owners confuse coughing with choking. Both cause the pet to forcefully exhale. With choking, the pet has difficulty inhaling. When coughing, the pet can inhale almost normally. Be careful to distinguish the two: attempting to give first aid to a pet who is merely coughing can injure the animal.

First Aid for Poisoning

If you suspect that your pet has consumed a substance that is poisonous, look for evidence (i.e., an open container, a pool of antifreeze, etc.).

Call your veterinarian or a poison control center and be prepared to answer the following questions:

•   What product caused the poisoning and how much was ingested?

•   When did the poisoning occur?

•   What symptoms are your pet exhibiting?

•   Can you retrieve a container or label from the poisonous substance to determine the active ingredient?

Follow the instructions of the veterinarian or the poison control center.

If you cannot get in touch with a veterinarian or a poison control center, then induce vomiting with the following exceptions:

Do not induce vomiting if:

•   The animal is unconscious, semi-conscious, or convulsing,

•   There is evidence that the poison was: a strong acid, an alkali (such as bleach), a petroleum product, a cleaning product, or the substance was ingested more than 3 hours ago.

If your pet ingested one of these substances, or the poison was ingested more than 3 hours ago, it is imperative that you somehow get him to a veterinary facility for treatment.

To induce vomiting:

• Give full strength (3%) hydrogen peroxide by mouth at a dosage of 1 tablespoon per 15 to 20 pounds of body weight, or syrup of ipecac (follow label directions)

If the pet is going to be transported to a veterinary facility, search for containers of the poison to take with the animal. Transport the pet immediately: don't wait until vomiting commences (if you induced vomiting). Cleaning out your car is a small price to pay for a successful outcome in a serious poisoning case.

If you have any doubts as to whether a substance is poisonous, call a veterinarian or a poison control center.

Antifreeze has a sweet taste that may be tempting to cats and dogs; its ingestion is potentially fatal.

Fractures / Injuries

Fracture: a break or crack in a bone.

Closed fracture: fractures in which there is no related external wound.

Open (compound) fracture: fractures associated directly with open wounds (the bone may be visible through the wound).

Dislocation: an injury to the connective tissues holding a joint in position that results in displacement of a bone at the joint.

Sprain: an injury to a joint, ligament, or tendon in the region of a joint. It involves partial tearing or stretching of these structures without dislocation or fracture.

What to Do

•   Before treatment, precautions should be taken to prevent biting injury to the first aid provider. Muzzle and or cover the head of the pet.

•   Open fractures should be dressed with a wet dressing applied over the opening and bone.

• If possible, the limb should be immobilized with a splint to prevent further injury. Use any of the following:

\-   A mountaineering splint (see section on Real Limb in splints).

\-   A splint fashioned out newspapers or magazines or coat hangers (see both sections on Splints).

\-   A splint made of sticks of wood supporting the fracture, fixed in place with tape or cloth.

\-   Any splint should extend past at least one joint above and one joint below the fracture site.

What **NOT** to Do

•   If the splint is difficult to apply or the animal objects, do not attempt splinting. Carefully transport him to a veterinarian.

•   Never attempt to set or reduce a fracture or try to push a protruding bone back into position.

A fracture or dislocation or severe sprain may be suspected when the animal suddenly appears lame on a leg, or picks up a leg and won't use it. They may also be suspected following any major fall or blunt injury. Obvious findings of a bone protruding from a wound are rare. What is more common is the unusual angulation or deformation of the fractured area, and swelling. Accurate diagnosis requires the use of x-rays.

An x-ray is the only way to accurately diagnose a fracture.

How to Move the Injured Pet

The first aid provider must not only identify and treat injury or illness, but must also safely transport the patient to the veterinary facility for treatment. Improper technique when transporting a patient can result in further injury or complications. Although a book of this type cannot fully prepare the reader for all specific examples, it can provide the following general recommendations.

Handle the Pet as Little as Possible

Try to make the pet comfortable by encouraging him to lie down and stay. Smaller dogs and cats can most effectively be transported in commercially available carriers or in a cardboard box with a lid.

Handle the Pet Gently

Rough handling may cause further internal bleeding, more damage to the soft tissues around a fracture, and many other complications.

Lie the Pet on its Side

If the pet seems to resent this or has more difficulty breathing on its side, it may indicate the pet has an injury to the chest or lungs. In this case, it is better to leave the pet in a comfortable position.

Minimize Movement

It is best in many cases to actually tie or tape the pet to a flat surface. This is imperative when handling the unconscious patient or the patient with a suspected back injury.

Do Not Put Pressure on the Stomach

This is most important for the pet who is having difficulty breathing, has been vomiting, or has pain in the abdomen.

Use a Backboard

If the pet seems paralyzed or unable to get up, a spinal injury is suspect and the pet must be firmly immobilized to prevent further damage to the nerves. Get a firm, flat support (an ironing board, a piece of plywood, a collapsed cardboard box, a table leaf -- think of one in your house before you need it). Grasp the skin over the back of the neck and over the small of the back and gently slide the pet on to the support. Try to keep the back and neck straight. Tie or tape the pet to the support.

Position the Head

If the pet is unconscious, position the head in normal alignment with the body. It should not flex abnormally downward nor extend excessively upward. Improper flexing or extending can cause decreased blood drainage from the brain and cause serious damage. If the pet has vomited or appears likely to vomit, put the head down below the level of the heart. This will allow the vomitus to run out of the mouth and not down into the windpipe and the lungs. Be aware that pets with severe head injuries are likely to vomit, even while they are unconscious.

Cover the Patient with a Blanket

Covering an injured pet has a calming effect. More importantly, it prevents heat loss. A blanket can also be used as a transport device if there is no sign of back injury. In this case, the animal can be gently lifted with the blanket. Gently slide the pet into the center of the blanket.

Roll the edges of the blanket to provide a better grip. Gently lift the blanket and the pet into the transport vehicle. This is usually a two-person procedure.

Know the Route to the Veterinary Facility

Get precise directions and drive directly to the facility. This will result in the fastest delivery of the pet for professional care.

Drive Carefully!

Driving out of control or in a panic may result in delays (while the officer writes a ticket) or injuries if you are involved in an accident.

Emergency situations require prompt and safe transport of the sick or injured pet. If done properly, this will give your pet a better chance for recovery. If delayed or done carelessly, the outcome may be less favorable. As with most first aid principles, prior planning and awareness of proper techniques will prevent many problems.

First Aid: A Final Note

Most veterinary hospitals are not open around the clock. Some may provide emergency service (meaning someone will meet you there if you call first). If you do not call first, you may arrive to find that a doctor is not available. To avoid wasting time in a crisis, ask your veterinarian ahead of time about emergency services available, and learn the shortest route to your veterinarian and to the 24-hour emergency facility, if one is available in your area.

Hyperthermia (Heat Stroke, Heat Prostration)

The elevation of body temperature above normal. It is sometimes indicative of a fever, but it can also be associated with severe conditions such as heat stroke or heat prostration. Any time the body temperature is higher than 106 degrees, a true emergency exists.

What to Do

•   Remove the pet from the environment where the hyperthermia occurred.

•   Move the pet to the shade and direct a fan on him.

•   If possible, determine rectal temperature and record.

•   Begin to cool the body by wetting with cool (not cold) water on the trunk and legs. It is helpful to use rubbing alcohol on the skin of the stomach and allow the fan to speed evaporation.

•   Transport to a veterinary facility.

What NOT to Do

•   Do not use cold water or ice for cooling.

•   Do not overcool the pet.

•   Do not attempt to force water orally.

•   Do not leave the pet unattended for any length of time.

In the summertime, other than fever, the most frequent cause of hyperthermia is heat prostration or heat stroke. Most of these cases can be avoided by following the advice in the Preventing a Health and Safety Crisis section. Keep in mind that prolonged seizures, eclampsia (milk fever), poisonings, and many other conditions may cause hyperthermia. Also, the bracycephalic (short-nosed) breeds (Pekingese, Chinese Pug, Lhasa Apso, Boston Terrier, etc.) may suffer from ineffectual panter syndrome (see the difficulty breathing section), which results in an increased body temperature that can be fatal.

The most common sign of heat prostration or heat stroke is vigorous panting. The pet is likely to be lying on its side, unable to stand, although some are restless and agitated.

There may be a thick, ropy saliva in the mouth, or froth coming from the mouth and/or nose. Often the pet seems to be rigid, extending its head, neck, and limbs.

The mucous membranes are often red but may be pale or "muddy." The pet may show signs of shock.

Rapidly cooling the pet is extremely important. While ice or cold water may seem logical, its use is not advised. Cooling the innermost structures of the body will actually be delayed, as ice or cold water will cause superficial blood vessels to shrink, effectively forming an insulating layer of tissue to hold the heat inside. Tap water is more suitable for effective cooling.

Severe hyperthermia is a disease that affects nearly every system in the body. Simply lowering the body temperature fails to address the potentially catastrophic events that often accompany this disorder. A pet suffering from hyperthermia should be seen by a veterinarian as soon as possible.

Impalement Injuries

Impalement injuries involve a foreign body stuck in an animal. Common examples in small animals include pets shot with arrows or crossbow bolts. Dogs frequently carry sticks in their mouths and suffer impalements when an end of the stick jams into the ground. Pets have fallen from multiple story buildings and become impaled on car radio antennas. A veterinarian should be seen as soon as possible.

What to Do

• Calm and blanket the pet.

• Attempt to immobilize both the foreign body and the pet. Severe and continuing damage is done whenever the foreign body is allowed to flail about the inside of the pet.

• If the foreign body is in the chest, listen for sounds of air sucking around the wounds. If it appears that there is an open wound in the chest, cover the wound (and the foreign body) with plastic wrap.

Apply petroleum jelly or antibiotic ointment before the plastic to help seal the wound.

• If the foreign body can easily be cut, shorten it, leaving only 3 to 6 inches sticking out of the pet.

What NOT to Do

• Never try to remove the foreign body yourself. In the case of a car antenna, cut the antenna from the car and take the pet to a veterinary facility.

Near Drowning

Suffocation by drowning is caused by the filling of the lungs with water or other fluid.

What to Do

• Remove the pet from the water.

• Place him on his side with his head and neck extended. It's preferable to have the head slightly lower than the body.

- Pull the tongue forward and expel any water from the lungs and stomach by gently pushing on the chest wall and stomach.

- Begin CPR as required.

- Cover the pet to avoid further heat loss.

- Seek veterinary help as soon as possible.

What NOT to Do

- Do not fail to seek veterinary help just because your resuscitation is successful and your pet seems to be recovering. Numerous secondary complications (i.e., electrolyte imbalance, pneumonia, secondary drowning) can occur.

- Do not leave the pet unattended as he may be confused and wander back to the water.

Almost all cats and dogs instinctively know how to swim. Unfortunately, they also instinctively swim to the nearest edge of a pool to get out. This is usually not the right decision. Most animals are unable to get out of a swimming pool at the edge.

They must swim to a step. If your pet has access to a swimming pool, you must teach him where the steps are. If you do not and he falls in, he will swim to the nearest edge and attempt to get out until he either accidentally arrives at a step, or tires and drowns.

If your pet has access to a swimming pool, you must teach him where the steps are located

Nosebleed

A nosebleed is bleeding or hemorrhage from the nose.

What to Do

•   Notice if the blood is coming from one nostril (note which one) or both nostrils.

•   If the pet is sneezing, note how often.

•   Attempt to keep the pet calm. Encourage the pet to lie down and relax.

•   Place an ice pack (covered by one or more layers of cloth) or compress to the side of the nose.

• If the nose is bleeding profusely or the bleeding lasts more than 10 minutes, seek veterinary attention.

What **NOT** to Do

• Do not put anything up the nose. This will likely cause the pet to sneeze. Sneezing will dislodge a clot if one has formed and the bleeding will resume. A bloody nose in a cat or dog may be associated with foreign bodies (foxtail awns are common), polyps, infections, poisoning, bleeding disorders, or even cancer. It is a sign whose significance should not be underestimated.

Paralysis

Paralysis is the inability to voluntarily move a part or parts of the body. The paralyzed part (legs, neck, etc.) may be rigid or stiff or, more commonly, relaxed and flaccid.

What to Do

• Calm the pet. If necessary, cover with a blanket.

• Muzzle the pet if there is any danger of being bitten.

• Transport the pet using one of the techniques described.

What **NOT** to do:

• Do not assume the pet won't bite.

• Do not encourage the pet to move about.

• Do not medicate the pet unless instructed to do so by a veterinarian.

The inability to walk can develop suddenly (with or without history of injury) in dogs due to the rupture of an intervertebral disc, especially in certain breeds like the Dachshund. Paralysis of this type should be considered a life-threatening emergency and your veterinarian or an emergency facility should be consulted immediately.

Paralysis can also be associated with traumatic episodes such as falls, being struck by a motor vehicle, or fights with other animals.

When paralysis is associated with trauma, fractures or instability of the spine should be suspected. It is extremely important to immobilize the spine before and during transportation. This is covered in the Transport section.

Physical Exam Checklist for Pets

To identify an illness or abnormal situation, you must be able to recognize what is normal for your pet. You know your pet better than anyone else and will have to decide when an abnormal situation warrants professional help. Sometimes the condition is so serious it leaves no doubt. Frequently, the changes are subtle and it is important that they are recognized. Early recognition of a serious problem can save your pet's life. The following pages teach you how to examine your pet and determine what is normal.

The primary suggestion is to give your animal a "mini" physical exam occasionally when there is nothing wrong so you get used to what is normal for your net. Record the normal values using the guide at the end of this section.

Hands-on Physical Exam

Before starting a hands-on exam, stand back and look at your pet for a few minutes. The posture, activity level, and general appearance can tell you a lot.

Now start the physical exam, making sure to look at the following areas. Consult a veterinarian if an abnormal condition exists.

A hands-on physical exam in the comfort of your own home is the best way to learn what is normal for your pet.

The Nose

Normal: Moist and clean Abnormal:

- Dry or cracked

- Nasal Discharge

- A moist or clean nose is a sign of a healthy dog or cat.

The Eyes

<u>Normal</u>

- Bright, moist, and clear.

- Centered between the eyelids.

- Pupils equal in size.

- Whites of the eye should not appear colored and should have only a few visible blood vessels.

- Pupils shrink equally when bright light is shined into either eye.

- Pupils enlarge equally when the eyes are held closed or the room darkened. Abnormal

- Dull, sunken eyes. Eyes that appear dry. Thick discharge from eyes.

- One or both eyes not centered.

- Pupils unequal in size.

- Abnormal colors that indicate problems are yellow (jaundice), brownish ('muddy'), or red (bloodshot).

- Pupils fail to respond or respond differently when bright light is shined into either eye.

- Pupils fail to respond or respond differently to the dark

Pay close attention to the color of the whites of your pet's eyes, as well as his pupils' response to changes in light

The Ears

<u>Normal</u>

- Skin smooth and without wounds.

- Clean and dry.

- Almost odor-free.

- Typical carriage for breed.

- Pain-free. Abnormal

- Wounds or scabs on skin. Lumps or bumps on skin. Any sign of rash.

- Crust, moisture, or other discharge in ear canal.

- Any strong odor from the ear.

- Atypical carriage for breed; for example, a droopy ear in a breed with normally erect ears.

- Painful.

Your pet's ears should be clean and odor-free.

The Mouth

<u>Normal</u>

- Teeth are clean and white.

- Gums are uniformly pink. Abnormal

- Tartar accumulation around the base of the teeth.

- The gums are red, pale, inflamed, or sore in appearance.

Press on the gum tissue with your finger or thumb and release quickly. Watch the color return to the gums. This checks the capillary refill time (CRT) and is a crude assessment of how well the heart and circulatory system are working.

<u>Normal</u>

• The color returns to the gums in 1 or 2 seconds (normal CRT). Abnormal

• The CRT is extremely rapid (less than 1 second) or slow (more than 2 seconds). Gums should be pink -- teeth should be clean and white.

Neck, Chest, and Breathing

<u>Normal</u>

• It is difficult to hear the pet breathe at all except when he is panting.

• The chest wall moves easily to and fro during respiration.

- Most of the act of breathing is performed by the chest wall. The abdominal wall barely moves.

Abnormal

- Any unusual noise heard while the pet is breathing could indicate a problem, especially if the noise is new for the pet.

- There is noticeable effort by the pet to move the chest wall.

- The abdomen is actively involved in the act of inhaling and exhaling.

Gently feel the chest and neck for any lumps, bumps, masses, or mats of hair which may be indicative of a problem.

Normal

- The pet does not change respiratory pattern while being palpated. Abnormal

- Palpation of the chest or neck seems to cause pain or discomfort. Any lump or mass you feel in your pet's neck or chest may be indicative of a problem.

The Abdomen

Palpate the abdomen. Start just behind the ribs and gently press your hands into the abdomen, feeling for abnormalities. If your pet has just eaten, there may be a palpable enlargement in the left part of the abdomen just under the ribs. Proceed toward the rear of the pet, passing your hands gently over the abdomen.

Normal

• No lumps, bumps, or masses.

• No discomfort on palpation.

• No distension of the abdominal wall.
Abnormal

• Any lump, bump, or mass may be abnormal.

• Palpation causes groaning or difficulty breathing. Any evidence or indication of pain is a serious finding.

• The abdomen feels hard or tense and it appears distended.

Any pain felt during an abdominal palpation could be a problem. Consult your veterinarian.

Skin Turgor Test

The test most often used to determine whether an animal is well hydrated (has enough fluid in its system) is the skin turgor test. To perform this, pull the skin over the chest or back into a tent and release it quickly (avoid the skin of the neck as it's often too thick for this Test). Observe the skin as it returns to its resting position.

<u>Normal</u>

• The skin snaps back into position so fast that the eye almost can't detect it. Abnormal

• The skin returns slowly or remains slightly tented. This is a sign of possible dehydration (see the dehydration section). The simple skin turgor test can tell you a lot about your cat's or dog's hydration.

Pulse and Heart

Learn to locate the pulse on your pet before a crisis. The best place on a cat or dog is the femoral artery in the groin area. Place your fingers around the front of the hind leg and move upward until the back of your hand meets the abdominal wall Move your fingertips back and forth on the inside of the thigh until you feel the pulsing sensation as the blood rushes through the artery. Count the number of pulses in 15 seconds and multiply by 4. This will give you the pulse rate in beats per minute (BPM).

<u>Normal</u>

• Cats: 150 to 200 bpm (A relaxed cat may have a slower pulse.)

• Small dogs: 70 to 110 bpm.

• Medium dogs: 70 to 110 bpm.

• Large/giant dogs: 60 to 90 bpm. (A relaxed dog may have a slower pulse. Know what is normal for your dog before a crisis.)

• Pulse is easily palpated, strong, and regular. Abnormal

- Too rapid or too slow.

- Pulse is weak, irregular, or hard to locate.

Feel the heart beat with one hand while feeling the pulse with the other. Normal

- The heart and pulse are synchronized -- for each heart beat there is a pulse. Abnormal

- There is not always a match between the heartbeat and the pulse. This is a serious finding.

Learn how to properly take your pet's pulse.

Temperature

Taking your pet's temperature is an easy and important procedure and can be done with a glass mercury or a digital thermometer. Digital thermometers are easier to read and can be purchased at a pharmacy for under $10.

Rectal temperatures are more accurate than axillary (between the front leg and the body) temperatures. Lubricate the thermometer with petroleum jelly. Gently and slowly insert the thermometer into the rectum about 1 or 2 inches.

If it does not slide in easily, do not force it. Leave it in for 2 minutes, then read and record the temperature.

Normal

•   Temperature is between 101° and 102.5°.

•   The thermometer is almost clean when removed. Abnormal

•   Temperature is below 100° or above 103°.

•   There is evidence of blood, diarrhea, or black, tarry stool on the thermometer. It may be easier to take your cat's temperature if you have someone to help you. Normals: A Final Note

Know the normals for your pet. Record the results of your pet's home examination using the outline on the following page. Watch your pet closely so you know when something is wrong. Become familiar with these normals before a crisis so you can recognize an abnormal finding.

Normals for my Pets

My pet _____ has the following normal values:

Normal Weight: ___ pounds

Resting Heart Rate (Pulse): ___ beats per minute

Resting Respiratory Rate: ___ breaths per minute

Rectal Temperature: ___ degrees Fahrenheit

Normal Gum Color: ___

Normal Whites of the Eyes: ___

Poisoning

A condition that results from the ingestion, inhalation, absorption, injection, or application of a substance that causes structural damage or functional disturbance of the tissues of the body.

What to Do

To summarize:

• Try to get in touch with a veterinarian or a poison control center, and follow their instructions.

• If you can't get in touch with either and the poisoning occurred within the last 3 hours, induce vomiting unless your pet has ingested a petroleum product, a cleaning solution, or a strong acid or alkali.

• If the product is a petroleum product, cleaning solution, strong acid, or strong alkali, or was ingested more than 3 hours ago, you must get your pet to a veterinarian as soon as possible.

- If the pet vomits, save a sample of the vomitus for later inspection by the veterinarian.

- For accidental application of a chemical to your pet's skin, see chemical injuries.

What NOT to Do

- Do not give any liquid (other than the hydrogen peroxide or syrup of ipecac if inducing vomiting): they may move the poison into the body sooner.

- Do not attempt to induce vomiting in seizuring, confused, or comatose pets.

Preventing a Health and Safety Crisis

Nutrition and Feeding

Good nutrition is essential for a healthy pet. Nutrients in pet foods should provide what is needed for metabolic body processes and should help fight off disease.

Proper feeding habits with nutritious food on a regular schedule can prevent:

- Disease

- Nutritional deficiencies

- Irritation or malfunction of the digestive system Improper feeding habits can cause or contribute to:

- Obesity

- Dental disease

- Heart disease

- Liver disease

- Pancreatitis

- Arthritis

- Inflammation and/or bleeding in the intestines

Many animals die each year from such diseases. Avoid table scraps, high fat foods, and foods that cause choking. Your pets should be offered foods developed for them or recommended by your veterinarian.

Provide Plenty of Clean Water

All animals, especially the very young and the very old, are susceptible to dehydration and kidney disease if deprived of water, quickly leading to serious complications.

Nutritious food and clean, fresh water are important to your pet's health!

Avoid Vigorous Exercise after Meals

Vigorous exercise after meals can lead to a life-threatening condition called bloat, which affects all breeds of dogs, but large, deep-cheated dogs are affected more frequently. With early and aggressive medical and surgical treatment, 80% or more of these patients survive this horrible disease.

Safe Environment

Unsafe situations may occur in your pet's surroundings, even with animals who are confined to the house or an outside run.

A responsible pet owner should always have control of their pet and their pet's environment. Injury or death after being hit by a car or being attacked by another animal can be prevented if your pet is properly controlled. Your pet may be shot or injured if allowed to wander unrestricted. Controlling your pet and providing a safe home can eliminate several dangerous situations.

Temperature

Animals have more problems in hot environments than in cold. Pets can suffer heat prostration and die in a short period of time, even minutes, under severe conditions. Good ventilation is vital. Animals cool themselves by panting, which becomes inefficient in extreme heat, poor ventilation, or when dehydration causes a lack of moisture on the tongue. If it is absolutely necessary to leave your pet in the car, even for a short time, keep the windows partially open. In the summer, the car's interior can quickly rise to over 150°, and your pet's body temperature may rise to 110° or more, causing irreversible brain damage and/or death within minutes.

Exercise

Your pets need room to move around safely to get exercise. Provide an area with adequate room, shelter, and bedding that can be cleaned. Lots of space to exercise, some toys, and clean, comfortable bedding are some simple things that can add years to your pet's life.

Leash Choking

Confinement created by a chain tied to a post or a cable can result in death by suffocation if the chain becomes too tightly wrapped around the post or around your pet's neck.

Proper Identification

Remember to have ID on your animal; people will usually return your pet if your phone number is provided.

Also, if your animal is injured and transported to a veterinarian by someone else, the doctor can reach you for medical decisions.

Proper identification tags will help you recover your pet if he wanders off.

Electric Cords

Electric cords should be inaccessible to pets, especially puppies and kittens, who tend to chew on anything. A bite through the insulation can result in a serious burn, fluid accumulation in the lungs, or death (see electrocution).

Dangling electric cords are an irresistible (but dangerous) temptation to a playful kitten or puppy. Make sure all cords are inaccessible!

Choking

Many common household items can cause your pet to choke:

• String

• Needles & Thread

• Hosiery

• Garbage

• Balls

- Yarn

- Socks

- Bones

- Gristle

- Small toys

These items should be kept away from pets, as ingestion may cause foreign body blockages or injuries to the esophagus, stomach or small intestine. Make sure that small household items are kept in a place where your pets can't reach!

Poisoning

Accidental poisonings can be tragic. Guard against ingestion of:

• Garden Supplies: such as insecticides, fertilizers, and snail bait.

• Poisonous Plants: Many plants in their live or dried forms are toxic. Even food items like dried onions can cause problems in pets. Discuss potential problems with your veterinarian or check with the nursery or a more complete reference before buying plants.

• Pennies: Some pennies contain zinc, which can cause vomiting, anemia, and even death if ingested.

• Chocolate: As little as one ounce of unsweetened (Baker's) chocolate may poison a small dog. Milk chocolate isn't as toxic, and if ingested in reasonable quantities there is no cause for alarm. Many dogs, however, ingest unreasonable quantities and may be poisoned.

• Antifreeze: Antifreeze has a sweet taste to dogs and cats, and they may lick it off the ground. As little as one teaspoonful (easily available from a radiator boil over) can lead to irreversible kidney damage and death in a small dog or cat.

• Medications: Some medications that are safe for us are not safe for pets: Tylenol (acetaminophen) is deadly poison to cats; No-Doz may cause convulsions in both cats and dogs; Solarcaine may cause anemia in cats; Advil (ibuprofen) may cause kidney damage or gastric ulcers in dogs.

Ask a professional before administering drugs of any kind to your pet.

Travelling

Animals must be contained while riding in a car or truck. Cats jump out of cars quickly. Put them in well-ventilated pet boxes. Dogs can be trained to a seat belt. We recommend that dogs not ride in the back of trucks. In some states it is illegal for a dog to ride in the back of a pick-up truck without tethers. Besides the risk of injury from a fall, the dog may be killed in traffic. Even properly tethered dogs have little protection in the event of an accident.

If your dog must travel in the back of a pick-up, then he should be securely tethered in.

Regular Veterinary Check-Ups

Regular veterinary examinations will help avoid some preventable disease problems and permit early detection of others, thus facilitating treatment. Your pet should be seen by your veterinarian at least once a year. During the check-up regular vaccinations are given and the animal is given a physical exam, a dental check-up, and teeth cleaning.

Your pet's annual/ physical is vital to her continued good health.

Vaccination Programs

Many dangerous infectious diseases can be prevented or lessened in severity with a proper vaccination program. No vaccine is 100% effective, but regular vaccinations are the most effective way to prevent such diseases. Approved vaccines are available for the following diseases:

Dogs:

- Rabies

- Distemper

- Parvoviral Enteritis

- Coronoviral Enteritis

- Hepatitis Leptospirosis

- Parainfluenza/Bordetella

- Lyme Disease Cats:

- Rabies

- Panleukopenia

- Rhinotracheitis

- Caliciviral Pneumonitis

- Feline Leukemia Virus

- Feline Infectious Peritonitis

With so many formerly deadly diseases now preventable by vaccination, you owe it to your dog or cat to make sure she is up on her booster shots. Consult your veterinarian for the vaccines needed in your area and a proper vaccination schedule.

Dental Health

Dental problems that go untreated not only cause problems in the teeth and gums, but their effects may extend to other areas of the body.

- Infections from decaying teeth may spread directly to the sinus cavities or the eyes.

- Bacteria from dental infections and/or plaque accumulation may spread to the heart, liver, kidneys, or other organs.

Good oral hygiene and regular veterinary examination and treatment can eliminate dental problems.

Dental health and good overall health go hand in hand.

Prevention: A Final Note

Seek professional veterinary help immediately if your pet suffers an accident or illness. Getting help early prevents complications and more suffering. Waiting can only result in undue worry, serious deterioration of conditions, and make recovery more difficult.

Shock

What is Shock?

In 1872 S.D. Gross defined shock as "a manifestation of a rude unhinging of the machinery of life." A recent veterinary textbook defines shock as "the clinical state resulting from an inadequate supply of oxygen to the tissues or an inability of the tissues to properly use oxygen." Many attempts have been made to define shock, but because it is such a complex disorder, no single definition has been successful.

Shock and the Cardiovascular System

To gain a basic understanding of shock, one must first have an understanding of the normal cardiovascular system of dogs and cats. Envision the cardiovascular system as the closed circuit diagrammed on the following page, consisting of a pump (the heart) and a series of stretchable tubes (blood vessels).

The system is filled to capacity with a fluid (blood) which circulates through the tubes delivering fuel (oxygen and other metabolic substances) and picking up trash (carbon dioxide and other metabolic waste). In order to be efficient, the pump must be able to deliver a proper amount of the fluid and there must be enough fluid to completely fill and stretch the system of tubes.

An insult to any part of this system that results in lower fuel delivery, excess fuel burning, and/or excess waste accumulation may result in a condition analogous to shock. An animal who has been hit by a car is in danger of suffering life-threatening shock.

Shock will ultimately lead to involvement of the entire cardiovascular system and, if left unchecked, will result in the death of the pet. For example, if a pet has been hit by a car and sustains injuries that cause blood loss, there will be a deficiency in the fluid that carries fuel. The pump (heart) operates on this fuel. Since an inadequate fuel supply is being delivered to the pump, it begins to fail. As the pump fails, it is unable to circulate the fluid that is present, so even less fluid is delivered. Without adequate fuel, the blood vessels become inelastic and are less efficient in fluid movement -- again, less fuel. Eventually, these events will result in total collapse of the cardiovascular system and the death of the pet.

Causes of Shock

The most common causes of shock in our pets is trauma: e.g., fights with other animals, being struck by a car, and gunshots. Other causes include poisoning, insect stings, fluid loss from vomiting and/or diarrhea, infections, burns, and lack of oxygen caused by heart failure or obstruction of airways (pneumonia or choking, for example). Regardless of the cause, shock is life-threatening. Immediate identification is crucial.

The Circulatory System

Oxygenated blood leaves the heart through the left ventricle (A), and circulates to the body (F) through the arterial system where its precious oxygen is distributed. The deoxygenated blood then travels to the right atrium (C) and the right ventricle (D) of the heart, where it is pumped to the lungs (E) to pick up more oxygen. The newly oxygenated blood returns to the heart via the left atrium (F), travels to the left ventricle, and the circulatory cycle begins all over again.

Signs of Shock

Early Stages of Shock

- Bright red gums.

- Very rapid capillary refill time.

- The pet may be either excited or subdued.

- Rapid heart rate.

- Pulse not difficult to find.

Middle Stages of Shock

•	Gums appear pale or "muddy".

•	Abnormally long capillary refill time.

•	The heart rate is frequently above normal.

•	The pulse weakens and may be difficult to locate.

•	The pet will most likely be subdued, depressed and weak.

•	Respiration often shallow and rapid (but may be normal).

•	Rectal temperature often below normal (may be normal or even elevated).

Late Stages of Shock

•	Gums extremely pale or show a bluish discoloration, and are often "blotchy" in appearance.

•	Capillary refill time is longer (sometimes longer than 3 to 4 seconds).

- Heart rate is probably elevated and irregular, but may be normal or below normal as heart muscle begins to fail.

- The pulse will be very weak and difficult or impossible to locate.

- Respiration may be slow or rapid, shallow or deep.

- The eyes may take on a glazed appearance and appear not to focus normally.

- Mental condition deteriorates from depression to stupor to coma.

- Rectal temperature will be below normal, often critically so.

Treatment of Shock: What to Do

Successful treatment of a patient in shock involves prompt recognition of the signs, immediate initiation of first aid procedures, and safe and rapid transport to the veterinary facility for definitive treatment.

First aid procedures include:

- Providing adequate breathing (see CPR).

- Stopping blood loss (see bleeding).

- Immobilizing the pet.

- Protecting obvious fractures from further injury (see splints).

- Preventing loss of body heat by covering the patient with one or more blankets.

- Immediately transporting the patient to a veterinary facility for definitive treatment of shock and other injuries and illnesses (see transport).

Treatment of Shock: What Not to Do

Well-meaning pet owners often use first aid procedures that may seem helpful, but, in fact, may prove dangerous to the animal.

• Do not allow the injured pet to move about on his own. Walking about or any unnecessary movement (especially allowing the pet to jump in or out of the transport vehicle) may increase internal bleeding. Unnecessary use of muscles "burns fuel," which can be fatal to a patient in shock.

• Do not apply a heating pad to a sick or injured patient. He may suffer a severe burn. In addition, application of heat will cause the vessels of the skin to dilate. These dilated vessels require more blood to fill them and decrease the efficiency of the already failing cardiovascular system, resulting in worsening of the shock condition.

• Do not pour water (or anything else) into the animal's mouth. Animals in shock are weak and may inhale anything given by mouth into the lungs, causing a serious complication.

• Do not administer any medications (including aspirin or other pain relievers) unless instructed to do so by a veterinarian.

• Do not assume the pet is not in shock after an accident. Early, mild stages of shock are difficult to recognize, and the pet may deteriorate rapidly if not treated.

• Do not hesitate seeking veterinary assistance. Many injuries and illnesses that cause shock may cause irreparable damage in minutes. Any hesitation could mean the difference between a pet making a full recovery and a pet that cannot be saved.

Snakebite

When your pet is "struck" by a snake, it is best to assume it is a poisonous bite.

What to Do

• Immobilize the part of the animal that has been bitten by the snake. Try to keep it at or below the level of the heart.

- Keep the pet calm and immobile; carry if necessary.

- Seek veterinary attention as soon as possible.

- Try to retrieve the snake if it can be done without risk. It is sometimes helpful to identify the type of snake.

What **NOT** to Do

- Do not cut over the fang marks.

- Do not manipulate the bitten area any more than needed.

- Do not allow the pet to move about freely.

- Do not ice pack or tourniquet the area.

- Do not administer any medications except on a veterinarian's advice.

- Do not use electric shock on the area.

Snakebite is a complex problem. The severity and type of damage done by venom depends on the type of snake involved.

Some snakes have venom that causes severe shock and rapid death. Others have most of their effect on the muscles. Some venom is very concentrated and some require large quantities before damage is done.

The first goal in snakebite treatment is to keep the venom from circulating in large quantity throughout the body. However, keeping all the venom in the area of a bite (as with ice packs or tourniquets) may cause severe muscle damage. Antivenom administered at the hospital is the most direct and helpful treatment for your pet.

If your pet is bitten by a snake, assume the bite is poisonous and seek veterinary attention quickly.

Straining

Straining is a frequent and sometimes exaggerated effort to have a bowel movement or to urinate.

What to Do

•   Transport the pet to a veterinary facility for examination and diagnosis.

What **NOT** to Do

•   Do not delay getting the pet examined.

•   Do not administer medications unless instructed to by a veterinarian.

It is often difficult to tell if the pet is having trouble urinating or defecating. Most owners feel their pet is constipated when they notice him straining. Straining produced by constipation may be identical to straining produced by diarrhea. Therefore, treatment of an assumed cause of straining may be the opposite of what is actually needed. In cats, straining is often indicative of urinary tract infection. Cats sometimes develop a condition called FUS (feline urological syndrome) or LUTD (lower urinary tract disease) in which tiny crystals develop in their urine.

When there are too many crystals, the crystals can plug the urethra (the tube that empties urine from the bladder) and prevent the bladder from emptying. The bladder becomes distended and the pet strains to relieve himself. Without help, this pet may be in critical condition within 24 hours. Dogs may also have obstructed urinary tracts.

Many other conditions can cause straining in cats and dogs: an enlarged prostate gland; irritated bowels; cancer of the bladder or bowel; intestinal or bladder polyps; and more. This is why the simple act of straining should not be assumed to have a simple solution.

Sunburn

Sunburn is damage to the tissues caused by exposure to the sun's rays.

What to Do

• Prevention is much better than treatment. Keep your pets out of direct sunlight.

• If your pet must be in the sun, apply sunblock containing PABA only.

• If your pet has burned, apply liberal quantities of an aloe vera preparation.

What NOT to Do

• Do not apply any other form of medication without first discussing it with Your veterinarian.

Animals are usually covered by hair, fur, or pigmented skin that protects them from the harmful rays of the sun. Any circumstance that removes this natural protection may allow the pet to receive enough radiation to burn.

If your pet has a shaved or non-pigmented area, you may apply a sunblock that contains PABA as the active ingredient. Some sunblocks contain other drugs that may be harmful if ingested.

Small areas of skin which are unprotected may be permanently tattooed with a dark ink; temporary coverage can be supplied by using a black magic marker or laundry marker to color the area.

When Your Pet Cannot Breathe

Difficulty breathing is also called dyspnea.

Respiratory distress is recognized by increased effort to breathe; noisy breathing; cyanosis (a bluish tinge to the lips and mucous membranes); and an inability to inhale or exhale.

What to Do

•   Keep the pet calm.

•   Suction the mouth free of any fluid that interferes with breathing.

•   If the pet has choked on a foreign body, perform the Heimlich maneuver and/or a finger sweep (see choking).

- Perform rescue breathing if necessary (see rescue breathing in the First Aid for Choking section).

- If the pet is overheated, wrap him in a wet towel.

- Seek veterinary assistance as soon as possible.

What NOT to Do

- Do not upset the pet.

- Do not perform rescue breathing on a conscious pet.

- Do not give anything by mouth.

Dyspnea, or difficulty breathing, is a serious sign. Causes include heart failure, severe asthma (yes, dogs and cats do get asthma), allergic reactions, bronchitis, pneumonia, paralysis or obstruction of the trachea, poisoning, and many other conditions. It is imperative to get the pet examined to determine the cause.

A special condition called ineffectual panter syndrome warrants mention for dog owners who live in warm climates. It affects brachycephalic (short-nosed) breeds (e.g., English Bulldog, Pekingese, Chinese Pug). Because of the short nose, the soft palate can interfere with breathing. On hot days or in hot environmental conditions these dogs try to cool by panting vigorously and the soft palate interferes even more. This cycle continues until the dog is severely dyspneic and overheated. Cooling these dogs is imperative. Wrap them in a wet towel and move them to a cool environment. This syndrome is manageable only by protecting these breeds from heat or by surgically reconstructing the soft palate.

Wounds

A wound is any break in the continuity of the tissues of the body, either external or internal.

What to Do

Deep Wounds

• Stop the bleeding (see the bleeding section).

• Do not attempt to clean the wound unless instructed to do so by a veterinarian.

• Protect the wound from contamination by applying a water- or saline-soaked compress. Do not remove it until instructed to do so by a veterinarian.

• Immobilize the wound to prevent further damage.

• Provide shock care if necessary.

• Obtain professional veterinary care. Transport the animal with the affected area facing up.

Superficial Wounds

•   Stop the bleeding. Clean and bandage the wound as instructed in bandaging section.

What **NOT** to Do

•   Do not apply materials (other than those mentioned) to the wound unless specifically instructed to by your veterinarian.

Conclusion

Many other types of emergencies can, and do, occur. If you have questions concerning symptoms your pet is exhibiting, seek advice from a veterinarian.

Emergency centers (where after-hours care is provided), and critical care centers (where 24-hour care is provided) are becoming more prevalent. It is recommended that you know the location and hours of operation of the closest facility.

There may not be time for you to call first in some very critical emergencies, but in most cases a phone call to the emergency facility is a good idea.

If there are any questions concerning your pet's health, call your veterinarian or the emergency facility. They can make you aware of some of the possibilities.

Take Care of your pet and God, the One and Only, will take care of you!